Baby Bear
and the big fish

Story by Beverley Randell

Illustrations by Isabel Lowe

2

The bears liked to go fishing
down at the river.

"I can see some fish today,"
said Baby Bear.
"Here they come."

Mother Bear
went into the river,
and she got some fish.

Father Bear got some fish, too.
"We are good at fishing,"
said Father Bear.

"Where is a fish for **me**?"
said Baby Bear.

"I can see a big fish,"
said Father Bear.

"This fish is for me!"
shouted Baby Bear.

Baby Bear got the big fish
in the net.

Away went the fish.
Baby Bear and the fish
went up the river!

"Help! Help!" shouted Baby Bear.
"I'm going up the river
 with the fish!"

"I'm coming," said Father Bear.

Father Bear came back
with Baby Bear and the fish.

"Look at my **big** fish," said Baby Bear.

"I'm good at fishing."